Rita's Tips for
DOMESTIC BLISS

Rita's Tips for
DOMESTIC BLISS

Rita Konig

EBURY PRESS
LONDON

For Honor with love x

First published in Great Britain
in 2003

1 3 5 7 9 10 8 6 4 2

Text © Rita Konig 2002, 2003
Illustrations © Sam Wilson
2002, 2003

Based on material published in
Domestic Bliss.

A CIP catalogue record for this
book is available from the British
Library.

Ebury Press
Random House,
20 Vauxhall Bridge Road,
London SW1V 2SA

Random House Australia
(Pty) Limited
20 Alfred Street, Milsons Point,
Sydney, New South Wales
2061, Australia

Random House New Zealand
Limited
18 Poland Road, Glenfield,
Auckland 10, New Zealand

Random House (Pty) Limited
Endulini, 5a Jubilee Road,
Parktown 2193, South Africa

The Random House Group
Limited Reg. No. 954009

www.randomhouse.co.uk

Illustrations **Sam Wilson**
Design **John Round Design**
Editor **Claire Wedderburn-
Maxwell**

ISBN 0 09 189729 7

Printed and bound in China
by Midas

Contents

Introduction

With the success of *Domestic Bliss* we decided to do this mini-me version – a quick hit of domestic tips and morale boosters. If you are looking for a present for a friend, this should do the trick. It's better than a cheap bottle of wine and would make an easy gift for just about anyone interested in living well with a generous helping of frivolity.

I hope that you don't find this book too bossy, I hope that it puts a smile on your face and I hope that it inspires you.

love

Mita x

Substance is what a room needs, not clutter or particularly dramatic things.

CHAPTER 1

Blissful
Rooms

Bedrooms

With a neutral palette in your bedroom you can change the look every time you change the bed.

Remember that there are many little details that can be added to beds, which make a huge difference to the way they look and feel.

Make sure you have lots of pillows – everything must be so soft that you can totally sink into your bed.

Keep an eye out for pretty quilts and blankets to put over the end of your bed.

Antique markets are a great place to find old linen. Pillowcases are an easy thing to start with.

Be careful when buying antique sheets – check their size and how worn they are.

Most old sheets are narrow and ideal for 4 foot 6 inch beds. 5 foot and up are harder to find.

Always hold a sheet up to the light to see holes and wear. Don't buy it if it is very thin in places, or take it but expect a short lifespan.

Old tablecloths are beautiful, although some of them have so much fine embroidery on them that you would never want to use them on a table so put them over your bed instead.

Blankets edged in satin are the best. Finding some satin in the morning to stroke your toe on is one of life's simple pleasures.

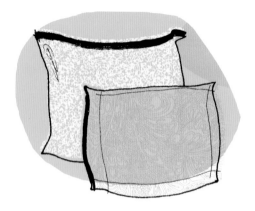

Don't have those big bedspreads that go over your pillows; they are so heavy and spend their lives on the floor. It is much more inviting to see the pillows on a bed – it just makes you want to jump on it.

Two large square pillows with two long pillows in front are best: you have always got to be able to throw yourself (or be thrown) on to your bed without cracking your head on either the wall or your headboard.

Guest Bedrooms

The more comfortable you make the guest bedroom, the more time your guests will want to spend in it. It takes the pressure off both parties to have to entertain one another all the time.

You must offer hanging space for guests or their room is just going to be so chaotic for the duration of their stay.

Don't overlook books beside your guest bed. The best thing is to have books of short stories or back issues of *Vanity Fair*, but change them according to your guests. I hate it when I have forgotten my book and find my only choice is some political biography that no one else wants to read.

Make the bedside table fantastically luxurious.

Make the guest bedroom really cosy and delicious.

Try to think of all the things you would like to have when you are away from home. I like to find a dressing gown, especially if I am encouraged to wear it for breakfast.

Leave a small decanter of whisky and a tin of good biscuits for your guest's midnight snacks, or a jug of water and a small bowl of some delicious fruit, such as figs, plums, apricots and grapes. Customise the snack to each guest.

There is much to be said for the approach of a chocolate on the pillow. If you can't quite get to grips with a Ferrero Rocher, break some squares off a bar.

Key things in guest bedrooms that are often overlooked:

- Make sure there are enough pillows, and make sure they are squishy. A single long pillow is by no means enough. Use square pillows if you have any – these are the most comfortable.
- A bedside light. There have been many times when I have had to grope my way from the bedroom door to the bed, stubbing my toes along the way.
- Extra blankets along the end of the bed look pretty, and mean that should your guest get cold in the night they can pull them up. As some people live in very warm houses and others like a slight chill, it is a good idea to offer the extra blankets.

Make sure you don't use the guest bedroom as a dumping ground.

If you don't have room for a cupboard think about using a panel of hooks instead.

A few covered coat hangers look pretty hanging from the hook.

The day bed option is very good for studies or if you have a room that you want to double as something else other than just a spare bedroom.

If you don't have a separate guest bedroom, then make the sofa in your sitting room as cosy as any real bed:

- Take off the back cushions, if it has any.
- Put a bottom sheet over the seat cushions.
- Put a duvet or sheets and blanket on the top.
- Use an end table or small chest of drawers as a bedside table and put lovely things on it, like a glass filled with garden or wild flowers.
- Make sure there is a lamp for your guest to read by.

Bathrooms

If you move and the bathroom is disgusting, try to budget to change it. It will never be a waste of money, and more importantly, you will actually enjoy having a bath.

Everything in your bathroom should be clean and fresh, so have candles and something delicious to put in your bath.

Candles in themselves are relaxing; in fact, the very act of lighting one sets a tone of calmness. They cast such a gentle light that this combined with their scent is a very good thing.

Ten Points for your Bathroom

1 Fill it with light. Use halogen spotlights and wall-mounted lights.

2 You will be dictated to a bit by pipes, but if the room is rectangular try to get the bath along the short wall. This will make the space more square.

3 Avoid having the loo right opposite the door.

4 If the bathroom is really tiny, think about a Victorian footed bath – seeing underneath it will create the illusion of more space.

5 Tile the walls to around shoulder height in white ceramic tiles. Choose whichever shape you prefer.

6 Paint above the tiles in a colour that you love.

7 Tile the floor in something different to the walls and try to have something that is not as slippery as glazed ceramic tiles.

8 Put up plenty of shelving near the bath for oils and scrubs.

9 Put up plenty of shelving around the basin for creams and make-up.

10 Put good stuff on the walls. Don't think you should not put your best things in the bathroom; it is, after all, the one room where you lie back and stare at the wall.

Guest Bathrooms

Making sure your guests find a lot of things to do in the bathroom is also going to give you some time to put your feet up.

To keep everything in order, use little and tall glasses. Q-tips and razors fit in short glasses or old demi-tasse coffee cups, and make-up brushes, mascara and lipsticks can be put in tumblers.

Put together all the necessities in your guest bathroom as well as delicious bath oils and scrubs.

The Perfect Bathroom Package

- Fluffy white towel, as large as possible.
- Smaller fluffy white towel for drying hair.
- A dressing gown on the back of the door – perfect for having breakfast in.
- Loofah.
- Bath essences and oils.
- Scrubs.
- Face masks – free tester sachets are perfect.
- Body lotion.
- Toothbrush.
- Toothpaste.
- Razors.
- Tweezers.
- Church candles.
- Alka Seltzer (depending on guest and proposed weekend).
- Shampoo.
- Nail files.
- Hairdryer.

NB Make sure there is always a wastepaper basket in your guest's bathroom.

Kitchens

For me, open shelving is the smartest. I love being able to see all my glasses and plates and they are so much easier to get at.

Rows of clean glasses and piles of plates and bowls are so great to look at, but this really only works with the stuff you use regularly otherwise they are going to get very dusty.

I like as much out as possible, and this goes for all the cleaning products as well – dishwasher tablets are my favourite because they have the nicest wrappers.

Drawers are always better than cupboards for pots, pans and large plates or dishes.

I like to keep all the brushes and sponges in an old china kitchen jar. Don't use glass though as the bottom will get nasty and marked from the dripping water and will never look pretty.

Have all those rolls of things like greaseproof paper, foil, cling film and kitchen towels sticking out of the top of a vase so they are always close to hand.

A mixture of plates can look beautiful on a table, but base your collection on a theme or it can become too much of a jumble.

Saucepans

1 If you have the space hang them from the ceiling on metal hooks over one of the work surfaces.

2 Keep them in a corner cupboard. They are a lot easier to cope with if you stack them with the lids on upside down.

3 Have them on open shelving. They are easier to get at and, more importantly, to put away.

Buy up old storage jars for your cereal, risotto rice and other dry store bits and pieces.

Washing-up liquid looks more attractive if it is decanted into a lovely bottle with an olive oil drizzle stopper pushed in the top.

Living Rooms

The most important thing in your living room is for it to be comfortable.

It can be very hard to work out furniture layouts when faced with an empty room. Don't panic and think about the following:

- Think of how your furniture works together in a social environment.
- Consider the function of the room and how many people you are ever going to have in there. It will help you enormously with where to put your furniture.
- Never leave a chair on its own, or a shy person will end up sitting there with no one to talk to.
- Put tables beside all the sofas and chairs as it is a real bore to sit down and have nowhere to put your drink.

Have a neutral palette on the walls and introduce colour through the upholstery and accessories. This way you can change the vibe with the seasons.

Try hanging a small picture very low down on the wall behind a lamp on a table. For little sketches and oils it gives the picture perfectly scaled-down surroundings.

Sofas

Make sure your sofa is deep enough and filled with a combination of about 60 per cent feather, 40 per cent down.

If you have upholstered your sofas in dark colours have an additional set of loose covers made in heavy white cotton for the summer.

There is something spoiling and extravagant about white upholstery.

One of the joys about loose covers is that they can just go in the washing machine when they get dirty, and the more haphazard and lived-in they look, the better.

Never buy a cheap sofa. It is a false economy, and if it is uncomfortable you will always regret it and want to replace it as soon as you can.

Make sure the cushions you get are really soft; they are not supposed to prop you up but to draw you in and envelop you.

Never rush out to find cushions and settle for the best you could find because almost the instant they are on the sofa you will see the thing that you really want.

Have big, fat, juicy, down cushions in the corners of your sofas with the smaller, plump ones in the middle.

When you puff up the cushions don't put them on the back of the sofa. Sit them square in the back of the seat – not in diamonds.

Pulling Power

Curtains are expensive, take copious amounts of fabric and keep out most of the light, while blinds cost a tenth of the price and are much slicker.

Don't have skimpy curtains as an economy because the material is expensive. Either have roller blinds made instead (2 metres compared to 16 metres!) or throw caution to the wind, choose a cheaper fabric and use two-and-a-half times the width of the window.

Blinds use very little material and are so versatile: they can block out the white sky, keep the sun out of your eyes, or just let all the light flood in.

Have dark blinds made for winter and then switch them for linen blinds in the spring.

Because blinds move up and down rather than from side to side it is much easier to get what you want out of them.

Having lighter weight blinds immediately changes the atmosphere because more light comes into the room.

Roller Blinds

- Have them made out of your own choice of fabric.
- Use slightly transparent material for the bathroom so you still have the light.
- Use a heavier material for a bedroom to block out the light.

Personalizing your Home

It is the details that make all the difference in life.

Mix and match. A room can look terribly tortured if everything is perfect and from the best places. You need that funny old lamp to keep it real.

Combine market finds, the dodgy wedding present and a splash of a different colour to create a unique room that no one else can copy.

Throughout the house there are things you can add and remove all the time and they all carry very different price tags and requirements.

Some items stand alone while others need to sit well with previous purchases.

Don't be afraid to mix generations and styles. Have good original detailing in a room alongside modern colours and furniture; modern art and antiques have always worked well together.

Remember the thing with style is that there are no rules.

Whatever you do, do it with confidence, and don't do anything by halves.

Whenever possible, try always to go for big and luxurious.

If you are nervous of getting it wrong, start off purist and let your style evolve.

Having loads of cash to throw at a room does not necessarily mean you are going to get it right.

Substance is what a room needs, not clutter or particularly dramatic things.

Your look will evolve. It takes a combination of things and time to create a good room. You can't rush it.

Make sure that what you have is comfortable, or you will just want to replace it

Remember that a badly made sofa will always make a room look awful, like an unmade bed.

Funky sofas are going to date very quickly, and you will be stuck with whatever fad was going on when you decorated.

Choose your upholstery fabric carefully.

If you have not done anything too dramatic with the sofa covers, you can change the look of the room really easily with different cushions.

Patterned sofas can look amazing, but patterns do have a tendency to go a bit 'posh-rental' on you, which is a really bad look.

Colour

Don't let colour terrify you.
Be daring and go with what you like.

Don't be afraid of getting bored of a wonderful colour. Use it – it will make you happy.

Be careful of using an amazing colour in every room. You need to strike a balance.

If you have any small spaces in your home fill them with mad colours that you are nervous of committing to in the larger rooms.

Paint the insides of the cupboards something crazy if you want to, it will make you smile even if nobody else ever sees it.

Colour combinations are important. Pure white can kill the warmth of a colour like dark red. You need a richer, more ivory white.

  Blissful Rooms

Choose good colours for the woodwork; often the window frames and the skirting boards get overlooked and are just painted in standard white. But you can do them in colours that look so much cooler.

Be careful of making a feature out of your woodwork. Instead, keep it tonal (and you will find that stronger colours can work in these areas).

How to Choose the Right White

- Painting different white samples next to each other on a wall is confusing as they read off each other.
- If you can bear it, it is easier to paint boards and look at them separately in the room, not necessarily against the wall.
- Whites can go quite peachy, pink or yellow. For me this is something to watch as they are smarter when they have a bit of slate or stone in them.
- If you are painting the floors white then choose a slightly different tone to the white on the walls. It stops it looking too like a light box.
- White-painted floorboards reflect the light dramatically so can really help dark rooms become cheerier.
- The easiest way to buy white paint for a room is from The Architectural Range at Paint Library.

Never feel that you have to use strong colours because you have to express yourself and it will make you more interesting or daring.

Always do the thing that works best, it may easily be that a pale colour is going to work better than a strong one in the space you have or with the things you own.

Remember that colours tend to come up much darker on the wall, and you won't even really get a sense of this by putting up samples of colour before you go ahead.

If you really love a colour, it is probably going to look fabulous.

Look at each possibility, listen to other people's advice but then, ultimately, do the thing that you prefer.

Remember that paint will darken as it dries, and when it is up on four walls each wall reflects the other, which means the colour becomes more intense. The same thing can happen in reverse, too.

It can be difficult to imagine what the colour is going to look like beforehand, so it can be a bit of a shock when you first see the room painted.

If you think you have got it wrong, wait a while. If after a couple of months you still hate it then change it.

Just because a room doesn't look how you expected, doesn't mean you aren't going to love it.

You will find that your eye for colour will develop very quickly.

For colour inspiration, look everywhere. The more you look at the colours around you, the easier you will find it to put things together and become quite daring.

You will soon learn which colours work well together – and which don't.

Details in your House

- They must not be overlooked.
- They need to be both frivolous and practical in equal measure.
- They need time. Never expect to have everything 'just so' instantly. It will look forced.
- Some of the accessories you add to your house will be 'finds': you won't necessarily know what they are until you stumble across them, and don't try to.
- Be prepared to spend a fortune on some accessories and virtually nothing on others. Never do anything in moderation.
- Details in the home are very often simply styling in the way you do things, from the

way you serve coffee to the way you make
your bed.

- Not all the details in your house need to
  be glaringly obvious. In fact, very often
  they aren't and either they remain things
  that only give you pleasure (very important)
  or, despite remaining un-remarked on by
  your friends, will ultimately add enormously
  to the overall look/atmosphere in your
  home.
- Don't over-detail as it can become quite
  over-powering.
- Don't ever do something for the sake of it,
  you have got to love it.

Space is usually quite precious,
so be clever with it.

CHAPTER 2

Solving Storage Problems

Storage

Practical is one of my least favourite words, but there are a few areas, such as storage, where practicality makes way for the good things in life. Your home can never be tidy if there isn't enough space to store the junk, and that will eventually drive you crazy.

When you are looking at homes, either to buy or rent, it is really important to look at what storage there is. Don't worry if there isn't any. See where you could put cupboards in and if you can't then think again.

If you own your property it is worth building cupboards because although it is an expensive thing to do it will be the saving of your sanity.

Space is usually quite precious, so be clever with it.

Your bedroom will never be tidy unless you can put your clothes away – hanging an old linen sheet in front of a hanging rail is not the answer.

Buy old wardrobes, which are beautiful, but as they tend not to have a huge amount of space they are generally better for men.

Old linen presses are lovely, and become more practical if you remove the shelves and replace them with a hanging rail.

Look at how much long hanging room you have compared to how much short, and how many folded things you own, so you can work out the cupboards accordingly.

Do not have cheap drawers. If your budget can't afford drawers then have shelves. Bad drawers will break.

You need to give your clothes space because if they are packed into a small space on wire hangers they will look awful very quickly.

The next time you buy something that breaks a new budget barrier, buy a decent hanger to keep it on. The cost of the hanger will seem small compared to the item.

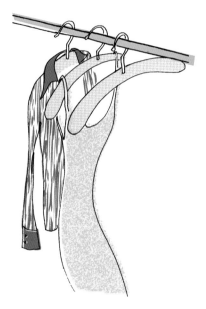

Solving Storage Problems

Deed drawers at the bottom of the cupboard can be a good way of using that void – home to broken shoes – that is the back of the cupboard.

Looking after winter clothes in the summer:
• Wash and dry everything.
• Place in zip-up plastic storage bags.
• Put the nozzle of the vacuum cleaner in the opening to suck all the air out of the bag so that it is vacuum packed. This will stop moths.

Preventing Moths

Keep lavender bags or camphor bricks in your cupboards as they will ward off moths and leave everything smelling delicious.

Change lavender bags once a year as they lose their smell.

Fumigate every six weeks if it is really bad.

Put conkers in your cupboards. The real bonus is that they don't smell, are easy to find and don't cost a thing.

Shoe Storage

Build shelves in the bottom of your cupboards for your shoes, like steps, or put in brass rods.

Make sure the rods are close enough together so your shoes don't slip in between them.

Keep shoes in boxes so they don't get dusty

- Either take a Polaroid of your shoes and stick the picture on the front of the shoe box.
- Or buy storage boxes in frosted or clear plastic that are the same size as a shoe box – you can then see the shoe.

Shoes need categorising in the cupboards. It just seems wrong for your wellies to be next to your party shoes.

  Solving Storage Problems

Extra Storage

There are many shops selling all sorts of boxes and cloth-covered cases, but you need to choose carefully.

Remember that you can keep a multitude of junk under your bed – but ensure it is organised junk, properly packaged.

The higher the bed, the less visual space it takes up in the room and the more room you have to store things underneath.

One of the joys of old brass beds is you can keep so much stuff underneath them.

You can keep a lot of things that don't need to be accessed too often in sealed plastic boxes.

Double a chest of drawers as a bedside table but make sure it doesn't come too far above your head when you are lying down.

If your bathroom is big enough you can always keep the sheets and towels in the top of a bathroom cupboard.

Trunks at the ends of beds are rather lovely and they hide a fantastic amount of things when they are not being used.

Piles of old suitcases are also good for storage and make very good bedside tables.

Solving Storage Problems

Organising and Keeping Linen

First, work out what not to keep. Remember to chuck out, give away or send down to the local charity shop regularly.

Don't throw away worn-out linen sheets – they make fabulous dish cloths. Don't cut them too small, because the fabric is thinner than a normal tea towel so you will need more of it.

Bundle up sets of spare sheets and tie them up with legal tape, which is inexpensive, can be bought in all legal shops and comes in pink.

Label the bundles with luggage labels so you know what is what (i.e. single or double sheets) and tie the labels with bows not knots.

If you are short of cupboard space keep sheets and pillowcases in sealed boxes under the bed, but make sure the boxes seal properly.

Bathroom Storage

No bathroom is complete without a large quantity of oils and scrubs. However, they do take up quite a lot of space and it is essential to have them within easy reach during your bath.

Put up glass shelves either beside or at one end of the bath.

Buy metal soap dish racks that attach to the wall and hang over the bath.

Built-in baths are good as they give you a bit of a ledge on which to put things.

For the things that you don't want on display use boxes. Find old tins in markets or use vintage perspex handbags.

Beside the loo have a jar for all your Tampax (there are some things that need to be kept slightly hidden but within easy reach).

I love an abundance of loo paper in a basket beside the loo. I have a slight loathing of loo roll holders.

Old luggage racks piled with spare fluffy white towels are very pleasing for the soul.

The Housemaid's Cupboard

Make a tall and skinny cupboard to house the ironing board, broom and vacuum cleaner.

Hammer in a pair of nails spaced a little less far apart than the width of the brush end of the broom, then just hang it upside down on them.

Vacuum cleaners benefit from having the long metal tube removed before putting them away, otherwise there is just far too much tubing – Boa Constrictor-style – for a normal person to deal with.

A large hook on the back wall to hang the ironing board on is pretty handy.

The Utility Cupboard

Utility cupboards incorporating a washing machine and dryer are a great alternative when you don't have the space for a laundry room.

Put your machines side-by-side with a counter over the top.

Paint the inside of the cupboard something delightful that pleases the eye.

If you keep the utility cupboard filled with lovely things, looking pretty, it will become a far less gruesome door to open.

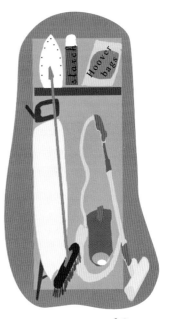

Keep everything waiting to be washed, dried or ironed in baskets on your counter.

Keep washing powders and liquids in the cupboards and then keep bed linen and towels on the shelves above.

It is a good idea to have quite a few shelves as it is best not to pile things too high, and it makes it easier to keep the cupboards tidy.

Essential Stock for the Utility Cupboard

- A large supply of vacuum cleaner bags.
- A good supply of all the light bulbs that you use.
- A stock of colour-run powders.
- Sellotape.
- Scissors.
- A ball of string.
- Extra plugs.
- A good supply of batteries.
- Super glue.
- A packet of screwdrivers. The best ones are the little packs with six different heads and one handle because in that way you don't lose the heads.
- An excellent bar of chocolate.

Storing Tools and Household Bits and Bobs

It is such fun putting boxes of things together. I am not sure what it is about having old shoeboxes on a shelf filled with useful things, but I love it.

From a styling point of view be particular about these boxes. Use favourite clear plastic shoe boxes for storage or smart old shoe/boot or bag boxes.

Solving Storage Problems

I find sewing baskets a bit of a pain – they are always a mess because the cotton threads are all in a knot.

For the toolboxes it is better when everything is a bit old and well used.

- Rags should be rags and not immaculately clean tea towels.
- Nails in the old jam jars should be a collection of old and new.
- Keep a few spare nails, screws etc. in little jam jars.

Always keep screw lid jars, particularly the ones that are good shapes as it is amazing just how handy they are.

Keep all your spare buttons in one jar; cotton reels in another; and another for safety pins and needles and a pair of scissors.

If you keep all your jars in boxes, label the lids so you know at a glance which jar you need.

Alternatively, just keep your jars on the shelf, sparklingly clean, minus all the labels and glue otherwise they look really ugly rather than pretty.

  Solving Storage Problems

Make sure you have a power drill in the cupboard so you will never be infuriated waiting for those small tasks to be done.

It's not rocket science – drill, screws and wall – so why do we assume only men can put up hooks and rails?

Storing China and Glass

How you store this depends entirely on how much you have and how much space you have.

Keep china and glass on open shelving if you don't have too much and use it regularly.

If you have a lot then build cupboards for it all. If you don't store it properly it is going to get chipped.

Have shallow shelving so you only fit one size of plate on one shelf, rather than stack them too high.

Cover the shelves in baize/felt. It comes in about a zillion great colours, so go crazy.

Keep your glasses upside down as it stops them from getting dusty.

Keep glasses in order of size and colour. Rows and rows of clean glass is one of the most beautiful things.

It is much easier to find the right number of glasses in the size you want if they are kept in an orderly fashion.

Clippings File

Magazines can start taking up a lot of space, so throw them out as soon as you have read them but after you have cut out relevant articles.

Clip out interesting articles as there is often stuff in magazines that is quite inspiring and you might want to refer back to it at some stage.

Clippings files are very useful for reference.

Divide the file up into sections, so you have colour schemes, floors, bookcases, flowers and exterior colours even if you think they are things that will never be useful.

Inspiration Boards

Pin boards are a very important thing to have in the office as they give your work space a little personality and they are a good way of reminding you of things.

If you get a postcard from a company that you want to be reminded about, don't file it because you will never look at it again.

Pin up anything that pleases your eye, and a random work of art will appear after a while.

Remember to edit the pin board from time to time as it can become rather a mess or boring.

Don't get dressed – do the housework in your underwear, it is much easier and the boys love it.

CHAPTER 3

Getting Around the Dreaded Housework

Domestic Chores

Coming home at night to a mess is deeply depressing, but it is only the dreariest of people who have everything immaculate all the time.

To stop menial tasks from becoming hideous you must strike while the iron is hot. Like all things that you don't want to do they carry enormous satisfaction value once they have been done.

Short cuts:
- Puff up the cushions on the sofas. Do it quickly before you go to bed or to work in the morning and the room will look 80 per cent better in a flash.
- If you don't have time to make your bed before you leave, pull it back and have the duvet or the blankets folded along the end of the bed with the pillows. It will air your bed and look relatively civilised.

Seven Ways to Make Housework Easier

1 Don't get dressed, do the housework in your underwear, it is much easier and boys love it; especially if you are in your best high heels. Plus flinging yourself round the place with Hoovers and dusters is hot business.

2 Do a home pedicure before you start. That way you can convince yourself that you are simply hoovering while you are waiting for your nails to dry.

3 Keep some treats in the laundry cupboard as this makes it very satisfying – I like to find some violet or geranium creams.

4 Have good music playing as loudly as possible – if you can successfully side-track your mind into singing and dancing you will hardly notice the chores.

5 Have everything for the housework in good order and well stocked.

6 Open all the windows to get some fresh air through the house.

7 Book a late lunch with a friend. A deadline is very important.

Getting Around the Dreaded Housework 71

It does not matter if you are not terribly ordered in the way that you clean. Chaos works for me.

Open all the windows before you start, or if it is cold outside wait until you have warmed up. It won't take long.

It is very important to air the rooms as they can get quite stuffy and also the cleaning products that you use stink.

Don't bother using air fresheners or sprays as that is not getting anything clean.

Be careful how you tackle dust as you can find yourself just moving it around the room.

At least once a week dust the obvious areas like all the tables and surfaces.

Getting Around the Dreaded Housework

About once a month dust the hidden areas that you forget about until you start to move any furniture – the tops of pictures, the window sills, the skirting boards, the bookshelves and the tops of lampshades and light bulbs.

Use damp cloths or these new wipes that lift the dust and keep it clinging to the cloth. There is hardly any point in doing it any other way.

Treats to get you around the House with the Duster

- Play good music for dusting, vacuuming or washing. Listen to Radio 4, or any talking station for the ironing – it's safer.
- Plan a lunch date at the end of it. You don't really need to do more than a few hours and a deadline really gets you going.
- Make sure you have elevenses. This is a treat in itself and one you can only really have when you are at home in the daytime. So break from the cleaning for a cappuccino and a biscuit or two.
- Hide some treats in the laundry cupboard, something you will forget about until you are doing the washing. It is good to reward yourself for such boring tasks.

- Run yourself a spoilingly hot and heavily scented bath at the end of your hours of cleaning. It serves a double purpose: it gives you a well-deserved soak and it will eradicate your bathroom of those horrid smells from the detergents.
- Scented candles are definitely a good thing to light at the end of a cleaning session so you can sit back and enjoy your clean and delicious smelling home.
- Remember to buy the papers or the latest issues of your favourite magazines so you can look forward to an afternoon lazing around the house going through them.

Making the Bedroom Lovely

In times of trouble and stress our bed is the place where we seek refuge, so it must be really luxurious – and of course, more importantly, it has got to be really lovely for the good times too.

Keep your pillowcases smelling good with linen spray or scent.

When making your bed, stretch the sheets as tightly as possible across the mattress as finding wrinkles is not great.

1 Fold the sheets at the corners in the same way you fold the corners of a present.

2 If you are looking at the end of your mattress with the sheets hanging over the edge, push the left side inwards, so you are left with the end of the sheet hanging straight.

3 Lift the corner of the mattress and fold it under as flat as possible.

4 Do the same with the right side. This is important, especially when you have a lot of blankets.

Cleaning Kitchens and Bathrooms

The kitchen and bathroom are really easy to look after. Because they are all hard surfaces it is just a question of cleaning products.

Kitchen

When you clean the oven make sure you rinse it properly, removing all the cleaning products, otherwise next time you cook in it people may think you are trying to poison them.

Don't overlook the fridge as it gets gross very quickly. Look out for those wipes for the inside of the fridge and microwave, which really do work.

Getting Around the Dreaded Housework

Bathroom

Scrub the whole bathroom, making sure all the windows are open.

Have an old toothbrush handy for those difficult-to-reach bits.

Once the bathroom is really clean, run a bath, which should signify the end of the morning's hard graft and time to get ready for lunch.

The trick with cleaning the bathroom is definitely in the products you use. I am not one for elbow grease.

Once a Month:

1 Take all your bath and body products off the shelves and polish the shelves.

2 Clean around the products' lids where they get gloopy.

3 Scrub between the tiles with a little bleach and then rinse thoroughly.

4 Pour limescale gel behind the plug thing on the side of the bath. This gets really disgusting and it is hard to get to. So pour the gel liberally and wait.

Cleaning

Cleaning Pans

Use wire wool and oven cleaner. Wire wool is to pans what a loofah is to the skin.

You can buy different softnesses of wire wool at most hardware stores on a roll, and it is also available with injected soap: the Brillo Pad made chic by Andy Warhol.

Cleaning Glasses

Sparkling glass is ravishingly pretty; dull, smeared glass does absolutely nothing for the eye. The only route to sparkling glass is a stack of very soft, dry linen cloths.

Washing by hand is a major bore, but machines aren't good for glass or crystal as they can make them squeaky or cloudy.

If you use a machine to wash glasses dry them off with a cloth or they will get a watermark around the rim.

To have gleaming glasses fill a sink with hot soapy water and add a little vinegar before washing your glasses. Then polish dry with a soft cloth – it will soon get them gleaming.

Getting Around the Dreaded Housework

Be careful of using very hot water and be even more careful of mixing the temperatures. If you are washing a piece of glass with hot water and then change the temperature to very cold it will crack. The glass equivalent of a heart attack.

Cleaning Decanters

Decanters and other similar-shaped bottles can be extremely tiresome to clean, just because it is so frustrating trying to cajole something out of the bottom of a bottle that you can't properly get into.

Use a bottlebrush if the neck is wide enough to permit it.

If the neck is too narrow use sand or very coarse salt, although the problem with salt is that in hot water it will eventually dissolve.

Put some coarse sand in the bottom of the decanter with hot water and washing-up liquid and swill it around. It will loosen any sediment and pour out quite easily.

To dry decanters:

1 Rinse with warm water.
2 Move the bottle around and around to create a whirlpool effect inside.
3 With a clever flick of your wrist, turn it upside down and the whirlpool will rinse the water out so the inside is left almost dry.
4 Dry the outside.
5 Roll up some kitchen towel on the diagonal to make a long tube (make it longer than the bottle) and leave it in the bottle overnight. This will remove the last traces of moisture.

If you put a stopper in while there is still any water inside you will get condensation around the neck and if that then dries it will stain and be almost impossible to remove.

Cleaning Silver
This is one of the most satisfying
of jobs.

Silver cleaning mitts don't really work in my
opinion and take far too much rubbing if they are
going to work at all.

Use the cream that comes in a tub with a sponge
and then rinse with warm water. You really do need
to get rid of all the cream.

If the piece of silver you are cleaning has any intricate
engraving or ridges you may need to use a soft toothbrush to remove the silver polish from these areas.

Make sure that you remove all traces of polish as beautiful silver objects will look ugly if they are still caked with polish in the difficult-to-get-to areas.

If you do scratch silver take it to a silversmith and he will buff it up for you and take out any dents. The only problem with this is that, of course, you wear the silver down a little every time you do it.

Don't put anything abrasive near silver as it is a very soft metal and you will scratch it.

Candlesticks

It doesn't take many candlelit dinners to positively clog up your finest candlesticks and little glass nightlight holders.

All you need are basins of piping hot water, which will loosen the wax so that it will simply drop off. Take care, though, because like hot fat you must not let hot wax just run away down the plug hole or you will be left with a blocked sink.

Make sure you leave enough space in the sink to run the cold water to solidify the melted wax, which you can then remove by hand and throw in the bin.

Give everything a good wash again with hot water and washing-up liquid to get rid of the greasy film that will have been left behind after the original soak.

Wax Dripping on the Table or Tablecloth

To get candle wax out of fabric iron it, using a very low heat, with some brown paper over the top of the wax. Be careful of using newspaper because if the fabric is at all wet you could end up with the day's headlines on your favourite cloth.

If you have a wooden dining table and do not always want to use a cloth to protect it or don't like non-drip candles there are two options:

1 Use the little glass collars that you can get to put around the base of the candle.
2 Use large mirrored coasters. You can find these in antique shops and they look beautiful on the table.

Be very careful of coloured candles over white cloths as wax is easy to remove but the dye is not.

Post-dinner Party Clear-up

If you can't bear to do all of it, just do the basic damage limitation.

However late, clear up that night, as there aren't many things that can make a hangover worse than a stack of washing-up interspersed with full ashtrays and old bottles of wine.

Ideally, have a friend stay with you while you do this; they are not there necessarily to help, but to sit, chat and do a general post mortem of the evening with you while you clear up.

Gossiping while you work makes the time fly by. There is something quite therapeutic about washing and chatting!

Once the kitchen has been cleared go back into the sitting room, puff up the cushions, and it's done.

Managing the Housekeeping

It is important to keep a tidy grip on housekeeping, especially all those household bills and appliance guarantees.

Have all your household bills and bank statements sent to your work so you can tackle bills while you are in that frame of mind.

Alternatively, keep the bills in files at home. As you receive bills put them in a folder and put them away, and then when you get your pay cheque sit down and pay them all at once and file them.

Clothes Washing

To make this task more appealing have:

- Beautiful clothes pegs.
- Deliciously spoiling scented waters for the iron and washing machine.
- Special non-detergent organic hand wash for your sweaters.

Hand washing is such a bore that it is so easy to be tempted to pop everything in the machine, but be careful because your underwear will eventually go grey and lose its shape.

Keep a few plastic basins in your bathroom for soaking clothes in overnight. These are best bought in light colours.

Getting Around the Dreaded Housework

Underwear

- Soak your knickers and bras before you go to bed.
- In the morning give them a quick wash, rinse them off and hang them out.
- Or rinse them in the machine on a 'delicates' option without any soap.
- Be careful with under-wired bras as their life span seems to shorten with all that spinning.
- Tights must not go anywhere near either the machine or the dryer as they will snag, so hand-wash those too.
- Wring tights out properly otherwise when you hang them to dry they will get longer and longer.

Wool

Wool needs special care, and there is a wool cycle on quite a lot of washing machines. Just take care when using it as clothes can easily be shrunk.

If you want to be safe then soak wool in cold water with a wool washing liquid overnight before rinsing and laying flat to dry.

Be careful wringing out heavy knits as they can stretch to oblivion. The water is so heavy that you should really wring it out before you lift them up.

The best way to wring knits is to lie them flat in the bath or sink and roll them up from there.

Alternatively, you can put knits in the machine to spin, which will keep the shape better than when you wring out by hand.

Make sure there are loads of hooks in the airing cupboard; the more things you can hang over the boiler to dry the better.

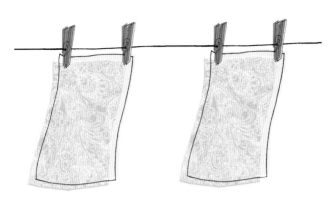

Nail a brass rod to the wall over the bath so you can gently steam your clothes while you are running a bath.

Some clothes can be hung in front of a window to take away the smell of cigarette smoke, which is better than spraying them with a product to mask the smells.

It is really important to keep clothes hanging out, but it is not necessarily a good thing to wash them or send them to the dry cleaners after every single outing.

Ironing

There is not much to say about ironing other than it is really boring and the horror of all the chores.

Don't use too much starch except on tablecloths. It is easy to chuck starch all over everything as it makes it so easy to iron, but it also makes your clothes really hard.

You can iron your sheets on the bed, just make sure they come out of the dryer a little damp.

Ironing linen and black crêpe needs careful attention as it will burn easily and go shiny.

Wool crêpe is light enough that you can just steam it.

Linen needs a heavy iron either:
- Iron it on the reverse side.
- Put a tea towel on top of whatever you are ironing to protect it.

Easy Ironing

- Iron in your nightie or knickers and vest, it is a hot business.
- Listen to the radio (a talking radio station is good), and the time soon goes by. Sadly, watching a film is not good as you can't look up much.
- Have one of Cath Kidston's ironing board covers as they are so pretty.
- Use a lot of steam.
- Use a spray can rather than the steamer part of your iron, which can splat black stuff all over your clothes.
- If using a spray can be careful you don't get a repetitive strain injury in your wrist and thumb area.
- Put a few drops of good-quality lavender water in the water sprayer. It makes your clothes smell delicious.

Sending out to the Laundry

If you send things to the laundry, keep a list of everything that goes out; they do lose things and it can be a while before you realise.

Keep a little exercise book listing things out and checking them back in again.

Make sure you get the same sheets back as it is not unheard of to be sent somebody else's sheets instead of your own.

If you are buying sheets from an established company it is usually possible to have an initial stitched somewhere on them.

Watch out that the sheets are not scorched – even the best laundries are quite rough.

Do not send out delicate pillowcases, do them at home.

As soon as you see any sign of scorching happening on your sheets, bring it up and start looking for a new service.

You may find that your laundry puts a little starch on the sheets when they are ironing and it is worth requesting that they don't as it makes the sheets too hard.

Dry Cleaning

Dry cleaning is basically a load of rather unpleasant chemicals being thrown at your very best clothes. This is why it is really not always the best thing to do.

If you have clothes with metallic or glamorous buttons make sure you cover the buttons in tin foil before the clothes are dry cleaned.

Leather can be a problem to dry clean and metallic leather particularly, as can any garment with things glued on, like sequins.

Look at the Care Label:

- If there is a P on it, which stands for perchloro-ethene, then regular dry cleaning should be fine.
- If there isn't one, or even a P with a cross through it, you need to find a specialist dry cleaner who does not use this process.

It is worth checking the label because dry cleaners will not take responsibility for very much. It is satisfying to have a little inside knowledge when dealing with people who assume you know nothing.

Inviting people to eat at your table is the ultimate way to seal a friendship.

CHAPTER 4

Blissful Entertaining

Entertaining

There are few things better than inviting people to your home – whether they are stopping by for a drink, dinner or the weekend, the gathering of kindred spirits in the comfort of your home is what it is all about.

I really believe that inviting people to eat at your table is the ultimate way to seal a friendship.

Offering people food and drink when they come to your door is one of the most basic customs of hospitality.

The Perfect Hostess

This sounds pretty scary, but the 'perfect hostess' should:

1 Not turn into some extraordinary form of Stepford woman.
2 Remember to have a laugh.
3 Remain your friend.
4 Be quite laissez-faire about her guests.
5 Be fairly relaxed.
6 Put a good group of people together.

Informal Suppers

Don't worry too much about how many guests you ask, people always flake at the last minute.

Invite one person who will set the date and from then on invite anyone you fancy.

Think of anyone you haven't seen for a while and would like to have over.

Whack out a few emails – it ensures mail and means you don't have to have a conversation.

On the day ring round the people that you mentioned it to, to check they are coming before you go shopping.

Organised or Formal Dinners

Don't be afraid of asking new people and keeping it to a number that fits around the table.

Work out carefully who you are going to ask.

The most entertaining and successful groups are usually when you get a bunch of people where everyone knows someone but no one knows everyone – the Daisy Chain Effect.

Don't put totally random groups around a table and be surprised when you get hideous silences.

You will know you have got the mix right when any of your guests makes friends with another at your house.

Weekend Lunches

The luxury of lunches at the weekend is that they can go on for hours and hours, because you never have to be anywhere else.

Make a very good Bloody Mary – mix Bloody Shames (no vodka) and add the vodka to taste.

For lunch you can have things that are heavier to eat and so easier to prepare than at dinner such as shepherd's pie or lasagne.

Let the afternoon ramble on and then you can either end up at the cinema or go for a long walk.

Meet walkers with a good tea when they get back – a very large teapot and hot buttered crumpets are ideal.

For Casual Dinners

1 Create an air of excitement around your invitations to prevent your guests from cancelling. It is good if there is a bit of a buzz and people look forward to it.
2 Never go to buy the dinner until you have confirmed the number of guests.
3 Think about over-inviting so you are left with the right number of people once half of them have blown you out.

Last-minute cancellations are extremely tedious. It is laziness on the part of the guest. It is one thing that really annoys me.

The Perfect Week

Sunday Cinema or cosy plate of spaghetti with a good friend.

Monday TV supper. This can either be alone or with someone else. If you are alone this is made a lot better by preparing something delicious for yourself. Come home, have a lovely hot bath, get into your nightie, light some scented candles and a fire (if you have one), get a video as there won't be anything good on TV, and cook a delicious dinner.

Tuesday Definitely time to get people over. Tuesday is really the dreariest of nights. Keep this easy, just a couple of friends for a low-key supper.

Wednesday If you are a half-full (as opposed to half-empty) sort of person this is definitely the eve of the weekend. This is an excellent night to entertain as you will find that people think of it much more as a dinner party than coming around for supper.

Thursday This is the night to have a party if you are thinking of having one. People are pretty relaxed about staying up late and still being able to scrape themselves through Friday in the office. It is better than a Friday when you lose quite a few people who might be going away for the weekend.

Friday Friday night is most definitely the going out night. Don't do anything at home, get your glad rags on and go and celebrate the end of the week with a couple of martinis in a glamorous hotel bar with friends, and see what happens.

Saturday Saturday lunch is a real treat as you can spend all afternoon sitting around gossiping with a girlfriend or boyfriend. Saturday lunch does not have the group mentality that a Sunday lunch has.

Sunday Sunday lunch with a whole pile of friends, newspapers and Bloody Marys has got to be the best thing ever, hasn't it?

Declaring Disasters

When it all goes pear-shaped in the middle of a dinner party:

- DO NOT cry.
- Declare disasters, but always with a smile. (Like the oven has blown up but you are dialling for a pizza.)
- Remember that the weird thing about the English is that they love disasters, so try not to worry when it all goes slightly off-track.
- Do something about it, as it is only a real disaster when you think that if you ignore the problem no one else will notice it either.
- Take some time out. Get into the kitchen and start doing something therapeutic, like the washing-up.

After-dinner Drinks

If you are a non-cook then the coffee tray is your chance to shine, because it all comes down to shopping and styling.

To make elaborate coffees the most easily appealing thing to do is to serve coffee in glasses rather than coffee cups.

For cappuccinos buy a mini-electric whisk for your hot milk or a creamer, a metal jug that you heat the milk in with a flat mesh whisk that you plunge up and down.

Soya Latte

For the non-dairy crowd. Heat the soya milk and froth to your heart's content.

Cappuccino

The fun part of making a cappuccino is the bits and pieces that go with it. Rather than sprinkling chocolate powder on top of the cappuccinos grate some chocolate or nutmeg.

Latte

This is phenomenally easy: simply froth up the milk, pour it into a tumbler (remembering to leave some space for the coffee) and then pour the espresso over the top.

99 Latte

This is very silly, which makes it irresistible. It is a regular latte in a stemmed glass with a flake standing up in it.

Sambucca

Sambucca is delicious in coffee. Serve the coffee in a tiny tumbler, and then splash in the sambucca afterwards. You could substitute the sambucca for Tia Maria or Sherridan's.

Vanilla Essence

This is not only delicious but a good non-alcoholic extra. It is good with espressos, cappucinos, lattes or macchiatos. Alternatively, serve vanilla sugar alongside your regular coffee.

Macchiatos

Make in small glasses as you would a latte, so you have a very dark drink with a perfect band of white froth at the top. For a healthy little affectation, add a twist of lemon to the rim.

If you have a little demi-tasse or two and would like to be able to show them off, give them to your guests with a piece of chocolate casually positioned on the saucer.

HERBAL TEAS AND INFUSIONS

You don't have to be restricted to coffee for total carried away-ness. Choose one or two flavours that you would like to serve and offer those. Better still, make a pot of one and offer it at the table.

Using Flowers

You can buy camomile flowers and vervaine leaves in some health food shops and delis.

Canarino

This is Italian for hot water and lemon rind. Peel the rind off the lemon in one go so it sits like a lemon without a centre at the bottom of your tea cup.

Ginger Tea

This is an all-round winner. Slice some raw ginger and put it in a tea pot with boiling water. Or you can use ground ginger – for a cup you need a generous pinch of ground ginger and for a pot you need a couple of teaspoons, but it depends on your own tastes. You can mix it with a little lemon as well.

SUGAR
Violet sugar

There are really two types of sugar to serve with coffee, the old-fashioned coffee sugar and La Perruche brown sugar lumps.

Brown sugar is rather beautiful in its random lumps.

It looks even better if you scatter some crystallised violets between the lumps in the pot.

Blissful Entertaining

Vanilla Sugar

This is a fun thing to serve with coffee. Either buy it in a specialist cooking shop or put a vanilla pod in the sugar.

Be careful that the bowl of sugar doesn't look manky when the vanilla pod gets sugar stuck to it. The point of vanilla sugar is for it to be pretty and delicious and old-fashioned, so remember to keep it looking lovely.

After-dinner Chocs

It's a good idea to have something sweet at the end of dinner with coffee; just when you think that it is all over, something more arrives.

It does matter how treats present themselves at the end of dinner. This does not mean that they always have to be smart, they just have to be thought about.

Do not go for sub-standard chocolates. While there are times when a box of Terry's All Gold is absolutely the thing, there are also times when it is better to look at bars of chocolate for inspiration.

A bar of Green & Black Almond Chocolate takes some beating. Just crack a couple of bars and put them down on the table.

Little chocolate bars are easy to put on the tray because you can stand them up in a glass.

Remember the old favourites from your childhood – like Tunnoch's tea cakes and snowballs – and your guests will gasp in admiration and child-like joy.

Smart chocolates are not out of the question, but they are not necessarily to be kept for your smartest dinners. Cheap chocolates are, equally, not necessarily exclusively for cosy suppers.

There is nothing more spoiling than a box of Charbonnel & Walker being passed your way or a yard of Bendicks' Bittermints.

Non-chocolate Treats

Never think you have to do anything by the book – you can do anything you like differently to anyone else.

In winter, sweet dates and Biscotti are good

The best reason to give a party
is for the hell of it.

CHAPTER 5

Perfect Parties

Parties

Planning a party is almost the best part about it – who to invite, what you are going to wear, the food, the drinks ...

Plan it with a girlfriend because two heads are definitely better than one to bounce ideas off.

Jointly organising a party also gives you more confidence, enabling you to ask people you don't know all that well and giving you a wider pool of friends.

Details are critical and every single one will be noticed and loved.

When to have a party:

- Celebrate in the drab and boring months of the year because that is when people are the most up for it and will leap at the chance to get dressed up. January is an obvious time.
- Valentine's Day is waiting perfectly in February to be celebrated. Also lots of people hate it and long for a distraction.
- If you feel you would like to have some sort of celebration to attach to your party then find something frivolous, like the first day of autumn.
- Don't have a Christmas party as you will be stuck at your own party while everyone else is skitting in and out of several others around town. There is also so much competition.
- Remember the best reason to give a party is for the hell of it.

The Considerations

There are reasons for and against having a party at home depending on:

- Your attitude towards your home.
- How many people you want.
- How much you care about maintaining good relations with the neighbours.

All are overcome-able:

- Get over the new carpet.
- Don't panic about the numbers.
- Invite all the neighbours (they probably won't come).
- Move all the rugs around the room into temporary spots, then move them back over the stained areas and you will be left with the beautiful protected areas.
- Remember if you put people in a beautiful environment they will behave accordingly.

Important Things for a Good Party (in order of importance)

- The music.
- The people.
- The drink.
- The lighting.
- The atmosphere.
- Door policy. Don't have scary bouncers who are going to be rude to your friends. If doormen are necessary, tell them to let everyone in and if they are not on the list, to ask them the names of the people giving the party so that at least you know they are not going to cause trouble.
- Don't panic about gatecrashers too much.
- Enter the party spirit and have fun and be pleased that other people want to come.
- Be very careful of gatecrashers who haven't come with your friends. They can be quite light-fingered.

Planning a Party

Make a list, putting boys down one side and girls down the other as this is the easiest way to see how even the balance is.

Don't panic when you have more boys than girls, or vice versa. It nearly always works out in the end – it is common to have a 10 per cent fall-out on the day of the party.

Invite people you don't know terribly well. Never be nervous of this. Everyone loves being asked to parties.

Make sure you have a good mix of people, and be slightly aware of people knowing one another.

Make sure you don't have a bunch of people who know each other intimately and then throw in one new person.

The best groups are always the ones where everyone knows at least one other person but not every other guest.

The Music

The music is so important: it will make or kill your party.

Choose carefully – remember how many times you have heard people complain about the music at a party, or say that it was brilliant because the music was good.

Seven Ways to Prepare for a Party

1 Move all the furniture and rugs out of the way.

2 Make sure there are lots of places for people to sit.

3 Create lovely little corners, which are ideal areas for flirting and gossiping.

4 Make sure you have enough clear surfaces for people to put their drinks on.

5 Make sure you put out enough ashtrays on the tables.

6 However much you hate smoking, you have to give in and go with the flow when you are hosting, otherwise all the most entertaining people will be huddled in the garden. It's as simple as that.

7 A detail that goes down really well is pots of cigarettes and, although not to be promoted, it does have a kind of 1930s glamorous cigarette box feel about it.

Flowers

Flowers are an especially lovely detail and quite important.

Go to the market on the day of your party and buy them cheaply and in bulk. Don't go for fancy arrangements.

Have huge vases of the same flower.

A vase packed with daisies is a delight.

Also use bud vases that just take one or two stems. They don't cost much to fill, and make a huge difference to the room. They are particularly good on small tables in the gossipy/flirty corners.

Go for bulk, there is nothing sadder than mean-looking vases.

Get the scale right. Three sunflowers in a huge vase of water look wonderful and probably better than a huge bunch.

Only fill the vase one-third to one-half full with water.

Tulips should be bought in bulk as one bunch is never enough, unless you are putting them in small vases.

Have a few small vases – pint glasses are useful and so are single tumblers.

Grouping small vases and glasses of different heights and shapes looks really pretty.

Don't feel you always have to keep to the same colours, usually it is best not to, there just needs to be a spirit that gives some continuity. Threes are a good number to use.

There are so many cheap and good-looking vases on the market, but be aware that a 'good value' wide-necked large vase can cost a lot of money to fill.

The Big Night

Get a few core friends to come early as it is dreadful being the first to arrive at a party, and it can be awkward for you too.

If your best friends come early they can calm your nerves and by the time the others start arriving there will be a bunch of people already drinking and chatting.

Alternatively, arrive late at your own parties. In this way you never have to worry about that stagnant moment at the beginning and it is lovely to walk into a full room, even if it is a little cheeky!

Tasty Treats
Try to do something a bit different. Everyone loves to be surprised.

Cosmopolitans are beautiful because they are pink, but they therefore do have their drawbacks.

Go for vodka-based drinks. You will rejoice every time you see one get knocked over as you will know that your careless friends are actually cleaning your carpet for you.

Make sure you have a lot of ice.

If you are having a lot of people get a barman. This may seem extravagant, but it is a nightmare if you have to act as barmaid.

Remember that your guests will always be as relaxed as you are.

Introduce people to each other, but don't drag people away from a good time to introduce them to someone they don't know.

Have little dishes of goodies on all the tables, which is much easier than having to keep passing food round.

Canapes

- Forget smoked salmon rolls unless you are having a 'nineties revival' as your theme.
- Try sushi; you can go down to your local Japanese restaurant and get take away – sushi is cold and easy to eat.
- Keep your eyes open throughout the year for other good things. Most foreign food is good for inspiration, for example Lebanese and Turkish.
- Think about having lots of different things, like vine leaves and chicken wings.
- Toast is great because there are so many delicious things you can put on top.
- Bake new potatoes and have 'Spud-U-Like' style canapés with a baked bean in the top or sour cream and caviar.
- Try a little British sausage with some mustard, or shrimp with cocktail sauce (not marie rose sauce, but tomato and horseradish).

The Post-party Blues

These are very common and understandably so. For months you have plotted and planned, invited, arranged and gossiped and giggled. Then it is all over.

Plan something for the following night.

Have a post-mortem dinner to pick over the party. You only need one friend and some leftovers for this.

Get over any minor damage; the burn mark in the middle of the mantelpiece and the red wine on the carpet come with the party territory.

Try not to find out who did it or it will colour your view of them and it is really not worth it.

Taking Presents

Presents do not have to be very dramatic – if you want to take something it only needs to be a token.

The key is for the present to be something unusual.

It is good to take something delicious to have with coffee, which is usually little and easy and doesn't interfere with dinner.

Instead of buying the standard box of chocolates, take a bar of flavoured chocolate (Rococo make black pepper chocolate and Earl Grey chocolate).

Presents should not be wrapped, but should be presented well, encased in a bit of tissue or popped into a cellophane bag.

If taking flowers, try to avoid ones that are not absolutely ready to go into a vase.

Tulips are good from the low-maintenance point of view because they have such a fabulously haphazard nature.

Often flower stands will have little posies of seasonal flowers like lily-of-the-valley or violets, and these are a delight to receive and lovely to give.

Go to any department store and set about spoiling yourself with new bath oils, scrubs and nail polish.

CHAPTER 6

Treating Yourself

Scenting
the Home

People always remark on walking into a house that smells good – there is nothing more welcoming than a good roast wafting from your kitchen.

The ultimate joy is to walk through your front door and be met with the cosy smell of home. So think about what that is when buying fragrances.

Watch out when you buy smelly candles as there is nothing worse than a cloying sweet smell.

Different seasons require different scents. White florals are best for spring; woods and spices for winter.

Pot Pourri

For entrance halls a bowl of pot pourri
is the best. It is like slow-releasing
vitamins and it lasts for ages.

Don't buy cheap pot pourri. Buy proper pot
pourri from a company that specialises in making
scented products. I am not talking about red and
green dyed cedar shavings mixed in with some
peach stones.

In my opinion, there are only two brands worth
buying: Agraria's bitter orange and Santa Maria
Novella's blend.

Buy a small bottle of 'reviver' to add as it loses
its smell.

To prevent pot pourri from getting dusty stir it up regularly, whenever you remember, as this brings the fragrance rising back up to the surface.

Know when to chuck out your pot pourri. Buy some more rather than letting it hang around.

Keep some by your sofa in your sitting room – every now and then it will let out a blast of deliciousness.

  Treating Yourself

Burning Essences
and Essential Oils

The alternative to candles is burning essence and essential oils.

It is worth making the effort to use the nightlight candle and a bowl of water as they smell fabulous.

Alternatively, the essences work just as well when put on a ring on a light bulb. Plus this is clean, safe and efficient.

Burning essences can be very strong so before adding more you should leave the room and then come back in to realise how strong it really is.

Essential oils (but not burning essences) are really excellent in the bath, but check the bottle because sometimes they are not suitable for the skin.

Essential oils also leave the bathroom smelling delicious for hours.

Burning essence is a very pure way of scenting the room.

Remember that you only need a few drops of essence!

Heavily Scented Flowers

Any heavily scented flowers make a good living alternative to dried pot pourri.

- Tuberoses smell divine and are ideal for the hall. They are not recommended for bedrooms.
- Freesias smell delicious. I think they are rather under-rated. You need lots of them as they can look a bit weedy.
- Hyacinths.
- Lilies-of-the-valley really mean spring has sprung, and what a scent they have!
- Jasmine will grow and grow if you look after it properly. It also has the most sophisticated scent, which is not too sweet or even too floral.

Finding the Right Scent for the Right Room

Different rooms require different scents.

Keep a few alternatives as your mood will reflect the scent you want around you.

Burn a couple of scented candles at the same time to create your own heady mix. Just experiment and if it smells dreadful, open a window and start again.

Jo Malone, England's premiere perfumer, has always recommended fragrance layering and the bathroom is the easiest room to do it in.

Remember, there are no rules, all you need is to be sure of what you like and keep it simple.

If using joss sticks do not economise as the smoky smell of cheap joss sticks is very studenty!

Burning joss sticks are best kept for winter or nights.

Fragrance is really no different to colour and should be viewed as the final decorating tool in a room.

Room Fragrances

For darker rooms (libraries, men's dressing rooms and sumptuous drawing rooms) use spices like orange and cinnamon, and woods like sandalwood.

For lighter rooms (chintzy drawing rooms or just paler palettes) use florals like geranium, hyacinth, orange blossom and roses.

For bedrooms use something gentle and calming like a citrus, floral, lily of the valley, lime blossom or even a little violet.

For a baby's room use something soothing like lavender, which is also a natural sleep enhancer.

For a cold winter night burn a tuberose candle in your bedroom or jasmine; these are much heavier smells that will envelop you.

Tuberose fills a room very quickly and can be mixed with a citrus smell such as grapefruit to lift it.

Scenting your Workplace

Remember that in your work place you should be surrounded by a good smell.

In your office use something that you don't have at home, especially something that you really love, as it won't be long before you associate it with your desk.

Use a scent – a citrus or woody fragrance is good, to create a positive atmosphere for all those people who are coming into your work space.

If your office smells good, you will be a couple of steps ahead in a meeting before you have even opened your mouth.

Use fragrances at work to reveal your personality, but keep them light and fresh.

Fat Saturdays

I defy anyone to say they have not had one of these. Even the skinniest of girls complain of bloated stomachs, dreadfully depressing swollen ankles, and low-on-morale days when the world is doing you wrong.

Find some cash so that you can spoil yourself.

Avoid all clothes shops with dodgy lighting in the changing rooms.

Head for beauty instead. Go to any department store and set about spoiling yourself with new bath oils, scrubs and nail polish.

Go and find some great things for the home. Markets are a good place to start.

If your current account is looking positively anorexic, you can compromise – just spend a small amount of cash and then head home.

Spend the day in your bathroom:

- Put on some good music.
- Get your bathroom smelling delicious and get some order in there.
- Sit on the floor and clean around all the tops of the bottles of lotions that have become clogged up and dusty.
- Chuck out every horrible sample that you have got free with a purchase and never used.
- Wash away all the spilt powder that is all over your make-up.
- Replace the junk with your new purchases.
- When you see all your bottles are standing ordered and immaculately arranged on gleaming glass, you will feel better.

Tidying your Home

Clear out the cupboards, but be sure not to be too dramatic.

Re-arranging what you do have is good for morale. Get your sweaters colour coded.

If there is a dearth of clothes in your cupboard, put the sweaters on hangers – they will look delightful and make you feel like you have masses to wear.

Organise all the skirts together and then all the trousers – start making it efficient.

Get the shoes that need repairing out from the black hole at the back and down to the menders. Make do and mend. It is so satisfying.

Polish your shoes.

Attack the chores that you have been putting off. Face them head on and you will feel marvellous by the end of the day.

Chuck out the piles of paper and things you have not been quite sure what to do with for years. If you have not done anything with them yet, you won't miss them.

1 Take to your bed – it is very good for you. But you need to feel like you deserve it so only do it at the end of your sorting.

2 Change your sheets even if you had clean sheets the day before; at times like these it is a frivolity you can afford.

3 Spend the evening tucked up with with a good movie or a book.

The Fridge

There are a number of particularly good staples to have in the fridge for a rainy day:

- Some good chicken stock (this will allow you to make a delicious risotto).
- A small pot of delicious pâté of confit for those gloomy evenings when you really can't be bothered to cook for yourself.
- Caviar is obviously good for a morale boost.
- Chocolate or sweets, for example Charbonnel & Walker violet creams.
- Treats that remind you of your childhood such as floral gums, snowballs, or a packet of sour strawberry laces.

Photos

The photo pile grows with the inevitability of a Labrador puppy, and unless taken in hand from the beginning grows into an out-of-control mess.

Rotation is better than re-decoration, it is cheaper and quicker.

If photo books seem too much like hard work, plaster the pictures all over the walls.

Find one area of wall where you can put pictures up.

Try attacking the photo albums when you are short of something to do and need a pick-me-up. Going through pictures of happy times is good for the spirits.

It is always good to see new things around the home, and an everchanging circulation of photographs is quite a good way of doing this.

Gather up all the photograph frames from around the house and empty all those photos that you have been looking at for years.

Go through the pictures sorting them out for albums, walls or photo frames.

Go through all the photos and write on the back who is in them and where you were together and when.

Do not be afraid to throw out any bad photos.

Start forming orderly piles and it will feel altogether less daunting.

Start off by putting the pictures you want to have out in the frames. This will get one job done quickly and easily.

To get the photograph albums sorted you need to be realistic; don't consider doing them all in one fell swoop.

Do each album trip by trip and before you know it the book will be done and you can move on to the next.

If you find the big albums hellish to have to tackle, it is much easier to buy the very small ones that take one picture per page.

Getting the Pictures on the Walls

The best places to do this are kitchens or bathrooms and the hall, depending on the size. Small walls are best.

If you have a big hall you are not going to make a big enough impact, so take the wall at the end and plaster it with pictures.

With a larger space, find yourself a patch to start on and give yourself room to grow around it.

You can also stick photographs in the sides of picture frames, which is really easy, charming and informal.

The bonus of putting pictures in the sides of frames is that if you get bored of the picture or person in it you can easily put another over the top!

Polaroids

There are several varieties of polaroid cameras and all are good.

The best thing to have is an old land camera because you get fabulously old-fashioned 4½ x 3½ -inch prints with a white border, failing that try the Fuji Maxi.

Polaroids are best for head shots as groups of people really get too small.

In the Office

Make your desk a good place to be. This is important as you spend the majority of your time there.

Put your stamp on things where you can, like your pens and notepads.

Never settle for standard issue stationery. Head to Muji and get yourself a Perspex desk kit; buy a bundle of shocking pink pencils and get the pen that you like.

Change the colour of your computer screen. Green is a good neutral colour that is easy on the eye; navy blue or dark purple is a lot better than black.

Obvious treats:
- A supply of chocolate biscuits.
- Getting a cake for tea.
- Ice lollies in the summer for all the office.

Wish Lists

Every time someone asks what you would like for your birthday or Christmas you probably wonder what to say ...

When you make a wish list you are not asking anyone for anything, they are for wishes, so you can add absolutely anything you like to it.

A Gull Wing Mercedes is perfectly acceptable as is the humblest of nutmeg graters.

The joy of a wish list is that you never have to ask for anything ever again.

Just copy your wish list when anyone asks and give it to them – they will have a broad selection of presents to choose from.

Wish lists are also just quite fun to make.

Camping should really be just one long, super de luxe picnic.

CHAPTER 7

Enjoying the Outdoors

Camping

The modern tent is the housing equivalent of a cagoule, and how compatible are nylon and nature in the ideal beautiful world?

Sleeping outside without a tent is the ultimate in camping. You run a bit of a risk, but if you want the outdoors, this is the best way to get it.

Take a bed roll with you and always remember your pillow.

Beech trees are the best thing to sleep under as their foliage is too dense for anything to grow underneath them so you will get the softest natural mattress.

Be prepared to be woken as early as 3am and start living in a different time zone to everyone else.

If you are not sure that camping with no cover is sensible then you can find a compromise between tented and open air camping with a bivouak.

If you can get your hands on an old army surplus, Swallows and Amazons-style tent then that is lovely.

It is all about the campfire, the rustling of leaves and the telling of ghost stories.

Camping Kit

- A bedroll including some drugget, blankets, sheets and pillows. Karamat comes highly recommended as it is thick foam, like a yoga mat, or take an inflatable mattress.
- A sleeping bag if you must. Try to find one of the ones that is nylon on the outside and brushed cotton on the inside for extra cosiness. They are very good for sleeping in a hammock.
- If not, a full set of linen sheets with blankets and eiderdown.
- A torch.
- Spare batteries.
- A box of matches.
- Cooking utensils.
- A good book.
- A guitar.
- Steritabs for purifying water.
- Smuggler fishing rod.
- Swiss Army penknife or a Leatherman.
- A compass and Ordnance Survey map.

Enjoying the Outdoors

How to Camp Indoors
There are times when it is necessary to camp indoors.

Camping indoors is best avoided if at all possible, and a month of it is about all most people can take.

Try to hold on to some standards and areas of luxury.

Make sure that your bed is comfortable and you have a bedside table, even if it is a box with a cloth over it.

Ensure your bathroom has good towels and plenty of things that will make you smell good in it.

There has absolutely got to be somewhere to sit.

Your life will be intolerable if you don't do the above things, even if it is going on in one room.

Dinner in the Woods

For the perfect Famous Five-style supper you have got to be near a river and be cooking a freshly caught trout.

Either cook your trout in tin foil in the embers of your campfire or on a skillet if you have managed to get the gypsy tripod together.

Keep your nostrils alert as you never know when you might stumble across some wild garlic, which is delicious to cook with.

Don't hold back on any of the things that are going to make your breakfasts, lunches and dinners delicious. Camping should really be just one long super de luxe picnic.

Make sure you either have 'one I prepared earlier' trout or a can of baked beans handy just in case the fishing is not fruitful.

Good camping food for the no-nonsense camper:
- Baked beans.
- Sausages.
- Eggs.
- Baked potatoes.
- Tea/coffee.

When you are on a camping trip there is really not much to think about other than what to cook next, so you might as well make it really good.

Good Camping Cooking Gear

- A gypsy tripod – this means that you can hang all the pots and pans over the campfire instead of burning everything in the campfire.
- A skillet for cooking on.
- A kettle.
- Pots and pans that can be hung from the tripod.
- Berlotti coffee pot.

Good Camping Food

- A Stilton.
- Full English breakfast.
- Some fresh herbs.
- A pepper mill.
- Olive oil.
- A lemon.
- A back-up fish.
- Some ready-made meals.
- Real coffee.

Enjoying the Outdoors

How to Build a Campfire

Everyone has a theory about making a campfire. It is one of those things, like a barbecue, that boys seem to feel they were born to.

Whatever the shape of the campfire you will need to dig a shallow pit first and fill it with dry leaves, bark and small twigs.

Dry fir cones are supposed to be the best and you should collect them while on country walks in preparation for camping trips.

Enjoying the Outdoors

The Tee-pee Method

1 Use young branches broken into lengths of about 8–13 inches.
2 Arrange branches like a red Indian's tent.
3 Light the kindling inside.
4 Once the sticks catch fire, start adding larger pieces of wood. It is important to build your fire gradually. Don't pack it too tightly because it needs oxygen.

The Log Cabin Method

1 Build a log cabin with branches until it is about 8 inches high.
2 Cover the top with more branches.
3 Light the kindling inside your log cabin.
4 Once the branches catch fire start adding larger and larger pieces of wood.

Alternatively, take a bundle of fire lighters and a blow torch.

Picnics
Winter

Winter picnics are rare treats that require careful thought.

Try:
- Delicious sausages.
- Spare ribs.
- Bananas wrapped in foil with melted Mars Bars.

Barbecues are great in the winter, and you can get throwaway barbecues.

Baby Weber barbecues are really good as you can just pop them in the boot of the car.

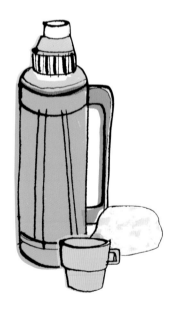

Spring/Summer
This is a really glorious time in Britain.

There are a few things that you can treat yourself with on a spring picnic like gulls' eggs, which are a seasonal treat.

Spring arrives around Easter time and if you are near the coast it is worth buying up masses of fish and lobsters.

High Summer

Instead of lying on woolly rugs use heavy old linen sheets, which are much more glamorous and comfortable.

Take delicious salads and bap fillings, along with some crab claws and cold bottles of wine, and more good treats.

The only real criterion for a good picnic is that it should feel as though the choices are never ending and that the leftovers aren't just being rolled out.

Why not have a fondue? All you need is a bottle of Kirsch, some cheese, a loaf of bread and a fondue set. It is certainly going to keep the cold out.

For a campfire put the fire in a big old enamel/ metal bowl. In this way you can take the fire away with you.

Picnicking on Foot

Buy a mini-Thermos flask, which is perfect for long walks.

Have a bunch of little bum bags for picnics. Fill them with:

- A mini-Thermos flask.
- An egg and bacon bap wrapped in foil to keep it warm.
- The compulsory treat.
- Boiled sweets – avoid chocolate because it melts.

Make sure you also take a camera with a good supply of film. A Polaroid is perfect for the instant gratification.

Cameras are great for children as they give them a purpose for walking and they will start to look around themselves, which we so often forget to do.

Picnics for Long-haul Flights

For long-haul flights a care package is a necessity.

Taking a picnic is far more civilized than eating from the airline tray. It will take time to prepare and get out and will taste far better than the airline food will.

Remember that whatever you take should be cold from the outset as hot things will be disgusting by the time you get to eat them and they also smell.

Don't take anything that requires a lot of cutting up. Either chop beforehand or take finger food.

As travelling takes its toll on your body so don't fill yourself up with unhealthy things.

Good foods for long-haul flights:

- Cold roast chicken. This is one of the best comfort foods and is both delicious and good for you.
- Salad. Also take some dressing with you in a jam jar.
- Pasta. This is very easy to digest and is highly recommended when you are jet lagged. Cold pasta salad is good.
- Chocolate or boiled sweets.

When booking flights on the Internet look at the food preference option as you will find food groups that you never knew existed, like low cholesterol, kosher with no carbs, Pacific rim, Oriental, Hindu and modern British; the list is quite extraordinary.

Picnics for Car Journeys

For long car journeys a good picnic is essential as the food opportunities en route will probably not be good.

Journey picnics are much better if they have been packed by someone else as it increases the lucky dip element.

Remember, it is much more fun packing a picnic for someone else.

Include all the things you long to get yourself when you unwrap your lunch.

Enjoying the Outdoors

Take pride in your picnics:

- Start by wrapping your sandwiches in greaseproof paper and tying with string, which makes a fabulous crinkling sound as you unwrap it
- Avoid tomatoes in sandwiches because unless you remove all of the pips and watery bit they make the bread awfully soggy.
- Put in little pots of mustard and chutney.
- Raw carrots and dips are good, too.
- Don't stock up on sweets.
- Treats are crucial as the whole point of a picnic is to find goodies that you weren't expecting, so a slice of cake and some chocolate must be in the bottom of the basket.

As there are so many different potential picnic occasions when on the move, approach each one individually.

Packed Lunches for School Outings

Why were other people's packed lunches always so much more exciting than your own?

Make sure your kids don't compare and despair the next time they have a packed lunch.

Unless you have one of those children who knows what they like and cannot see any point in trying anything new, put delicious new treats in there all the time.

Remember that fun-size packs of anything are never quite fun enough, so it is very important to add quite a few packs.

Enjoying the Outdoors

Don't always give your children healthy organic packed lunches. But at the same time don't always give them junk.

When your children only have packed lunches for school trips, it is very important to compete for the crown. E-numbers are good!

Index

About the Author

Rita Konig writes the cult column, Rita Says, in *Vogue* and also has a weekly column in the *Saturday Telegraph* magazine. Formerly weekly columnist for the style section of The S*unday Times*, she has also written for German AD, *House and Garden* (USA), *Traditional Home* (USA) and is the author of the bestselling *Domestic Bliss*. Rita also works as an interior designer. She is based in London.

About the Illustrator

After graduating in fine art Sam Wilson did an MA in illustration at Kingston University. Sam has since been commissioned by numerous clients throughout Europe for magazines, books, design and advertising. Last year she set up the Eye Candy illustration agency and moved to rural Staffordshire where she now combines illustrating with overseeing the agency.